The library is always open at
renfrewshirelibraries.co.uk

Visit now for
homework help
and free
eBooks.

We are the Skoobs and we love the library!

Phone: 0300 300 1188
Email: libraries@renfrewshire.gov.uk

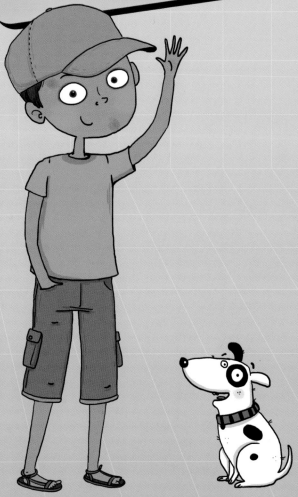

A Benjamin Blog
and his Inquisitive Dog
Investigation

Exploring Coasts

Anita Ganeri

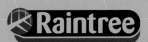
Raintree

Raintree is an imprint of Capstone Global Library Limited, a company incorporated in England and Wales having its registered office at 7 Pilgrim Street, London, EC4V 6LB – Registered company number: 6695582

www.raintreepublishers.co.uk
myorders@raintreepublishers.co.uk

Edited by Dan Nunn, Rebecca Rissman, and Helen Cox Cannons
Designed by Joanna Hinton-Malivoire
Original illustrations © Capstone Global Library Ltd
Illustrated by Sernur ISIK
Picture research by Mica Brancic
Originated by Capstone Global Library Ltd
Production by Helen McCreath
Printed and bound in China

ISBN 978 1 406 27105 8
17 16 15 14 13
10 9 8 7 6 5 4 3 2 1

British Library Cataloguing in Publication Data
A full catalogue record for this book is available from the British Library.

Acknowledgements
We would like to thank the following for permission to reproduce photographs: Getty Images pp. 14 (E+/stockcam); 15 (© LRM Photography), 26 (Universal ImagesGroup); Photoshot p. 16 (© NHPA/Laurie Campbell); Shutterstock pp. 4 (© Mariusz S. Jurgielewicz), 6 (© Elena Elisseeva) 7 (© Galyna Andrushko), 9 (© Pavelk), 10 (© Richard Cavalleri), 11 (© alexmcguffie), 12 (© Robyn Mackenzie), 13 (© Liliya Krasnova), 17 (© Karin Wassmer), 18 (© Julian Weber), 19 (© LiteChoices), 20 (© Natursports), 21 (© David Evison), 22 (© Ignacio Salaverria), 24 (© Oliver Hoffmann), 25 (© David Young), 27 (© Sergei Butorin), 29 bottom (© David Young), 29 top (© Stanislav Komogorov); SuperStock pp. 5 (All Canada Photos/Darwin Wiggett), 8 (Robert Harding Picture Library), 23 (F1 ONLINE).

Cover photograph of the Twelve Apostles in Victoria, Australia, reproduced with permission of Shutterstock (© Ashley Whitworth).

We would like to thank Michael Bright for his invaluable help in the preparation of this book.

Every effort has been made to contact copyright holders of material reproduced in this book. Any omissions will be rectified in subsequent printings if notice is given to the publisher.

Some words are shown in bold, **like this.** You can find out what they mean by looking in the glossary.

Contents

Welcome to the coast!

Hello! My name's Benjamin Blog and this is Barko Polo, my **inquisitive** dog. (He's named after the ancient ace explorer **Marco Polo**.) We have just got back from our latest adventure – exploring coasts around the world. We put this book together from some of the blog posts we wrote on the way.

BARKO'S BLOG-TASTIC COAST FACTS

Coasts are places where the land meets the sea. Canada has the longest coast of any country at 202,080 kilometres (125,566 miles). If you straightened it out, it would reach five times around the **equator**.

Changing tides

Posted by: Ben Blog | 2 March at 11.15 a.m.

Every day, the coast changes because of the **tides**. Twice a day, at high tide, the sea floods on to the shore. Twice a day, at low tide, it flows back out again. I'm in Brittany, France, at low tide – a great time to explore the beach. At high tide, the water can easily cut you off from the land.

BARKO'S BLOG-TASTIC COAST FACTS

The sea never stays still. Waves are huge ripples of water that the wind whips up as it blows across the sea. When the waves crash on to the shore, this is called breaking.

By the seaside

Posted by: Ben Blog | 23 April at 12.14 p.m.

We arrived on the island of Hawaii, in the Pacific Ocean, and headed straight for the beach. It's covered in strange black sand that's made from crushed-up rocks from volcanoes. Sand is made when the wind and waves smash rocks, shells, and **coral** into tiny pieces.

BARKO'S BLOG-TASTIC COAST FACTS

Have you ever collected pebbles on a beach? They are often round and smooth. This is because they are rubbed and scraped against each other by the power of the waves.

Caves, stacks, and arches

From Hawaii, we headed to South Africa and the Cape of Good Hope. The Cape is a **headland** – a rocky piece of land sticking out to sea. It's been worn into this shape by the wind and waves. The wind and waves also carve out features along the coast, such as caves, **stacks**, and **arches**.

BARKO'S BLOG-TASTIC COAST FACTS

When waves wear away at cracks in a headland, they carve out sea caves. Fingal's Cave on the coast of the island of Staffa, Scotland, is named after a giant in Scottish legend. Yikes!

The next stop was Australia, to explore the Twelve Apostles. Here's one of the photos I took. These amazing rocks are sea stacks, and some of them are as tall as four houses. A sea stack forms when the top of an arch collapses, leaving behind a tall pillar of rock.

BARKO'S BLOG-TASTIC COAST FACTS

This stunning sea arch is on the island of Gozo in the Mediterranean Sea. It was made when the sea wore a hole between two caves on either side of the headland.

Cliff climber

Posted by: Ben Blog | 7 July at 11.11 a.m.

Cliffs are steep walls of rock that plunge into the sea along coasts. These are the White Cliffs of Dover in England. They are white because they are made from **chalk**. They have been carved into shape by the wind and waves. I went climbing to get a better look.

I am here

BARKO'S BLOG-TASTIC COAST FACTS

The highest sea cliffs in the world are back in Hawaii. To reach the lookout at the top, you need to climb for more than 1 kilometre (¾ mile). But there is a fantastic view at the top!

Blooming coasts

Posted by: Ben Blog | 31 August at 3.52 p.m.

It's tough being a seashore plant! At high tide, plants get covered in water. At low tide, they are left high and dry. Seaweeds, like this kelp I snapped, have root-like **holdfasts** for sticking on to rocks so that they do not get washed away as the tides go in and out.

BARKO'S BLOG-TASTIC COAST FACTS
Mangrove trees grow along the coast where rivers flow into the sea. They have special roots that stick out from their trunks. These keep the trees firmly fixed in the mud.

I spotted some clumps of this plant as I was climbing up a sand dune on the beach. It's marram grass, and you can't miss its spiky, green leaves. Its extra-long roots creep deep under the sand. They hold the plant in place, and they also stop the sand from blowing away.

BARKO'S BLOG-TASTIC COAST FACTS
Coconuts that fall from trees often drift far out to sea. They bob along on the water until they are washed up on another beach. There, they take root and grow into coconut palm trees.

Wet and dry wildlife

Posted by: Ben Blog | 2 October at 1.29 p.m.

We're on the Galapagos Islands.
I snapped this marine iguana. Marine
iguanas are the only lizards that live
in the sea as well as on land. They
feed on seaweed that grows on the
slippery rocks. Luckily, these iguanas
are strong swimmers and have long,
sharp claws for holding on.

BARKO'S BLOG-TASTIC COAST FACTS

Sea turtles live out at sea but come ashore to **breed**. Females dig holes in the sand and lay up to 200 eggs. When the tiny babies hatch, they head to sea. Many are eaten by crabs and birds.

Our next stop was the Skeleton Coast in Namibia. It's a brilliant place for spotting Cape fur seals. Tens of thousands of seals breed here in November. Visitors can view the mothers and pups from a walkway. But you don't want to get too close – the seals smell terrible!

BARKO'S BLOG-TASTIC COAST FACTS

Oystercatchers eat shellfish, such as limpets, mussels, and cockles. They use their long, pointed beaks to **lever** the shells open and get to the tasty snacks inside.

Rock pool life

Posted by: Ben Blog | 19 December at 2.00 p.m.

Rock pools are home to some amazing animals and are brilliant places to explore. Sea anemones look like blobs of jelly. When the **tide** comes in, they wave their **tentacles** in the water to catch small creatures to eat. When the tide goes out, they pull them back in again.

BARKO'S BLOG-TASTIC COAST FACTS

Limpets cling on to the rocks with their large, sucker-like feet. This stops them from being washed away. For a better grip, they scrape a little dip in the rock to sit in.

Cracking up

Posted by: Ben Blog | 28 February at 1.48 p.m.

In many places, coasts are in danger. Here in Holderness, north-east England, I'll need to watch my step. Each year, about two million tonnes of rock from these cliffs crumble into the sea, taking people's cliff-top homes over the edge with them.

BARKO'S BLOG-TASTIC COAST FACTS
Coasts are brilliant places to go on holiday, but large stretches have been destroyed to make space for hotels, tourist **resorts**, and golf courses. Some coasts are now **protected**.

Crooked coasts quiz

If you are planning your expedition along the coast, you need to be prepared. Find out how much you know about crooked coasts with our quick quiz.

1. Which country has the longest coast?
a) Namibia
b) Canada
c) South Africa

2. What is black sand made from?
a) rock from volcanoes
b) crushed-up **coral**
c) smashed seashells

3. What are the Twelve Apostles?
a) sea caves
b) sea **arches**
c) sea **stacks**

4. How do seaweeds cling to rocks?
a) with **holdfasts**
b) with anchors
c) with suckers

5. Which lizards live in the sea?
a) chameleons
b) geckos
c) marine iguanas

6. How do sea anemones catch their food?
a) with their teeth
b) with their **tentacles**
c) with knives and forks

7. What is this?

8. What is this?

Glossary

arch feature along the coast made when the sea wears a hole between two caves

breed to reproduce, or have babies

chalk soft, white rock

coral rock-like material made by tiny sea creatures

equator imaginary line that runs around the middle of Earth

headland rocky piece of land sticking out to sea

holdfast root-like part that fixes seaweeds to rocks

inquisitive interested in learning about the world

lever pull apart with some effort

Marco Polo explorer who lived from about 1254 to 1324. He travelled from Italy to China.

protected saved from harm or damage

resort place where people go on holiday

stack feature along the coast made when the top of an arch collapses

tentacle long, waving body part that some sea creatures use to catch food

tide how the sea flows on to the shore and out again, twice a day

Find out more

Books

100 Things You Should Know about Extreme Earth, Belinda Gallagher (Miles Kelly, 2009)

Cliff Climbers (Landform Adventurers), Anita Ganeri (Raintree, 2012)

Coasts (Geography Wise), Jen Green (PowerKids Press, 2011)

Harsh Habitats (Extreme Nature), Anita Ganeri (Raintree, 2013)

Websites

environment.nationalgeographic.com/ environment/habitats
This National Geographic website covers a range of habitats.

www.bbc.co.uk/bitesize/ks2/science/living_ things/plant_animal_habitats/read/1
Learn about habitats on this BBC website.

Index